MARY
CHAFIN'S
# Original Country Recipes

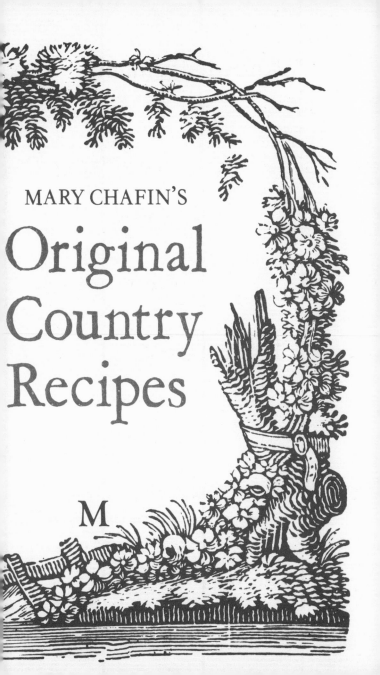

MARY CHAFIN'S

# Original
# Country
# Recipes

M

# Acknowledgements

The publishers would like to thank Major John Young, The Royal Artillery, for permission to reproduce the recipes in this book.

The historical research was carried out by Jessica Orebi Gann, and the recipes were tested and adapted by Nicky Hessenberg. Thanks are due too to Mary Ashby and John Tomlinson for advice on wines and cures respectively.

---

Design by Robert Updegraff
Picture research by Juliet Brightmore

First published 1979 by
Macmillan London Limited
London and Basingstoke

Associated companies in Delhi, Dublin,
Hong Kong, Johannesburg, Lagos, Melbourne,
New York, Singapore and Tokyo

Typeset by Filmtype Services Limited, and
Western Printing Services Ltd.
Printed by Butler and Tanner Ltd, Frome

British Library Cataloguing in Publication Data
Chafin, Mary
   Original country recipes
   1. Cookery, English
   I. Title
   641.5'942   TX717

ISBN 0 333 27381 8

# Contents

# Introduction

Mary Chafin's receipt book — leather-bound, the pages rather dog-eared but the handwriting surprisingly legible — contains a collection of recipes made over a period of several years, starting when her marriage was first planned in 1698 and probably continuing right up to her death in 1719. There are over 200 recipes for food and wine, and 135 potions. Many of the recipes are written in different hands and carry the name of the contributor; these range from immediate family and near neighbours to the notable families of several counties.

In addition to Mary's maiden name and the date, 1698, the flyleaf bears a pencil note that she was 'born at Chettle in 1680 and married William Clutterbuck in 1698'. This scant information was enough to begin a trail of discovery which led full-circle to the book's present-day owner and provided *en route* an intriguing picture of the social life of the time. (The results of this research may be found in the appendix on p. 78.)

Chettle is in north-east Dorset, on the edge of Cranborne Chase. The present Chettle House was not built until the early 1700s, and before that the Chafins lived in an Elizabethan house on the same site. The entrance to this would have led directly into the large hall, which was the family's main living and eating space. Bedrooms, a private parlour and possibly a long gallery would have been on the upper floor, and the servants' quarters above that. The kitchen would either have opened directly from the hall or have been a separate building. A large number of other outhouses would have provided for all the wants of what was virtually a self-contained community. The family and their servants 'brewed and baked, they churned and ground the meal, they bred up, fed and slew their beeves and sheep and brought up their pigeons and poultry at their own doors.'

In all this the women of the family played a vital part: wool and flax spinning, needlework of all sorts, embroidery, cooking, curing, preserving, wine-making and the preparation of herbs and medicines were all their responsibility, as the range of recipes collected by Mary Chafin demonstrates. Gardens were small and functional, largely devoted to herbs, and the importance of domestic remedies for common ailments is shown by the number of potions that Mary includes. Many of these use wild flowers, herbs and oils and are not unlike the 'natural produce' treatments in vogue today, but others cast a more sinister light on the nature of disease and the means of combatting it at the time, and some are positive witches' brews.

In 1698 Mary married William Clutterbuck of Exeter. The young couple appear to have continued to live on the Chettle estate for a while after their marriage, for the Chettle parish register records the birth of their first four children; but in 1709 they moved to Puncknowle (pronounced Punnel), a small village in south-west Dorset between Bridport and Dorchester. The Clutterbucks seem to have thrived in the early eighteenth century, and to have mingled with the noblest families in the South-West. Contemporary diaries suggest that as well as long visits from more distant friends there was much informal dining out on the spur of the moment. Dinner, the main meal, was eaten between 1 and 2pm, supper sometimes as late as 10pm. Beer was the most usual drink and every household brewed its own. Wines too were made at home, likewise cider and mead.

The period was one of intensive smuggling, largely of wine, from the French coast. Puncknowle, only two miles from the sea, was well known as a smuggling village — as Mary's references to French wine in her cooking suggest — but the influence of the new French cuisine, which abandoned medieval spices and oils in favour of lighter flavours, can hardly be

seen in her recipes. (The recipe for *crème brûlée*, however, is one of the earliest known in England.) The emphasis is on pickles and preserves, pies and puddings, and large cuts of meat. The cake recipes, apart from spiced fruit cake, are more similar to modern crystallised fruits than to cakes, and the biscuits are crisp fingers, probably intended for eating with the many fruit puddings. The puddings are one of the high points of Mary's cooking; they are deliciously rich, but even the fruit and suet puddings are not heavy because relatively little flour was used, while the fruit purees and egg puddings, including syllabub, are extremely good and desperately fattening. The eighteenth century knew nothing of cholesterol.

It is the gaps in Mary's repertoire which seem most curious to the twentieth-century eye. There are, for example, no salad or fresh vegetable dishes, and few of the recipes contain any vegetable at all apart from onions. One exception is the rabbit pie which contains artichoke hearts and either asparagus spears or a boiled potato (the only reference to potatoes in the book). She makes no mention of garlic, although it was certainly in use in England at the time. Vegetables occur mainly in pickled form, presumably to provide some variety during the long winter months when no fresh vegetables were available. This in turn suggests that fresh vegetables were used when in season, but possibly they were regarded as too mundane to be worth special treatment. The pickling recipes, which include mushrooms, cucumber and turnips as well as fish, all use a lot of vinegar and were judged too sharp for modern tastes.

One reason for the seemingly excessive use of vinegar was to disguise the taste and smell of meat that was going off (washing in vinegar and water is still a useful remedy for meat that has sat too long in its plastic wrapping and has begun to smell). Most of Mary's meat recipes, however, use lemon rather than vinegar, so are less sharp than the pickles, and the 'raggou' and fricassee are both excellent. Several methods of potting meat and fish are given, which would have been essential for those without any means of cold storage. The fish recipes are mainly for the oily fish caught in the Channel, such as mackerel and herring, and there are very few of them — perhaps because fish was eaten immediately and in its simplest form.

It seems fair to conclude from Mary's receipt book that her family ate extremely well, even though to our eyes their diet was somewhat unbalanced (several potions for the cure of scurvy confirm the lack of Vitamin C). Although her servants would have included a cook, a housekeeper and at least one housemaid, she would herself have been responsible for all the planning involved in keeping their large household fed and clothed throughout the year. It is perhaps not surprising therefore to learn that she died at the age of thirty-seven, although this was well over the average life expectancy of the time. May her recipes live on.

# A note on the recipes

The recipes have been tested and adapted where necessary to suit modern ingredients and utensils — an electric mixer was found to be particularly valuable in those recipes that recommend beating for two hours. Metric measurements have been rounded up or down to the nearest equivalent.

The quantities given by Mary Chafin for her large household have been reduced; most recipes serve 4–6. Eggs at that time were much smaller than our own, and numbers have been reduced accordingly. Anchovy essence has been substituted for fresh anchovies when these are required in small quantities.

Rose water and orange flower water, much used in the recipes, can be bought at the chemist rather than the grocer — once you have tried them you will not want to be without them.

We hope that the recipes in this book will enlarge your repertoire of dishes, and encourage you to experiment further with some of the excellent flavours lost to the modern kitchen.

# Meat

# To roast
# a Rump of Beefe

Take a Rump of Beefe that is fatt & young, salt it with salt, & let it lye three or 4 days, then stuff it very well with good store of sweet herbs, a pound of Beefe suett, half a dozen anchoveys minced very small, spitt it & lay it to the fier, first baste it with butter 'twill take six hours roasting, an hour & half before you take it up put under it a broad dish that will hold a quart of Clarett & half a pint of Elder vineagar, some butter, an oynion stuck with Clove, a couple of anchoveys put with the Clarett & keep basteing with that very often & what remains of basting the beefe add to it half a pint of good fresh gravy w:$^{th}$ some Oysters & Mushrooms, the quantity of both about a pint, stew them altogether & thicken it with the yolks of two or three Eggs, & putt it hott to y:$^{r}$ beefe in the Dishe——

A joint of beef, rubbed
   with oil and sprinkled
   with herbs
1 onion
½ pint (*300ml*) red wine
2 teaspoons anchovy
   essence

2–3oz (*60–90g*)
   mushrooms
2 egg yolks
Approx. ½ pint (*300ml*)
   good stock

Rub the meat with oil and sprinkle with sweet herbs.
Start roasting your joint as normal. About two-thirds of
the way through the cooking time put the joint on a rack
over the roasting tin. Pour over it the red wine and the
melted butter; mix in the anchovy essence and add an
onion stuck with cloves. Put the beef back in the oven
and continue cooking, basting frequently. When it is
cooked keep the joint warm whilst you make the gravy.

   Scrape up the pan juices and add the mushrooms,
peeled and chopped (and some oysters, if you can
afford them) and pour in the stock. Simmer for a few
minutes until the mushrooms are cooked, and then
thicken the gravy with the egg yolks dissolved in a little
of the stock. Stir continuously until thick. Pour into a
jug and serve with the beef.

# To make
# a rare Martlemass Beefe
### *Lady Lear*

Take a fatt Briskett of beefe & bone it, putt it into as
much water as will cover it shifting it 3 times a day for
3 days following, then take it out & putt it into as much
white wine & vinagar as will cover it let it lye in it 24
hours $y^n$ take it out & dry it in a Cloth & season it with
mace Nutmeg Ginger & Cloves beaten small mingle
with it a good handfull of white salt strew it both sides
of the beefe & rowl it up as $y^u$: would brawn, tye it up
as close as you can & put it into an earthen pot cover it
over with coarse paste, sett it into the oven with
household bread, keep it in the pott to eat cold, but pour
off the Gravy while it is hott put clarified butter over it,
& eat it with Mustard & Sugar——

| | |
|---|---|
| A joint of brisket | Ground cloves |
| Ginger root | Salt |
| 2–3 blades of mace | White wine |
| Grated nutmeg | |

Soak the joint for at least 24 hours in a mixture of white
wine and vinegar to cover. Next day mix some chopped
fresh ginger root, mace, grated nutmeg, cloves and salt.
Press this into the surface of the beef and put into an
earthenware pot or casserole with a tight-fitting lid.
Cook in a slow oven (275°F, gas no. 2) for $2\frac{1}{2}$–3 hours.

*This produces a very rich stock, and is delicious either
hot or cold. If eating cold, pour off the liquor and allow
the meat to cool in the pot. Serve the jellied consommé
with the meat.*

## Butchery.     *Lanionia.*

| | |
|---|---|
| The Butcher, 1. | *Lanio* 1. |
| killeth | mactat |
| fat Cattle, 2. | *Pecudem altilem*, 2. |
| (The lean 3. | (*Vescula* 3. |
| are not fit to eat) | non sunt vesca) |
| he knocketh them | prosternit |
| down with an Ax, 4. | *Clava*, 4. |
| or cutteth their throat | vel jugulat |
| with a slaughter-knife 5 | *Clunaclo*, 5. |
| he fleaeth them, 6. | |
| and cutteth them in | excoriat (deglubit) 6. |
| pieces, and hangeth out | dissecatque, |
| the flesh to sell | & carnes |
| in the Shambles 7. | in *Macello* 7. |
| | venum exponit. |

*Martlemas or Martinmas (11 November) was the day on which cattle were killed before the winter because of lack of fodder.*

5

# To dress Beef Stakes

Take buttock beef & cut it in thin slices, & chop it as you doe for Scotch Scollops wash them all over with Eggs on both sides $y^n$. strew them over pretty thick with Crumbs of bread mixt with sweet herbs, a little pepper & salt, fry them with very little liquor for the sauce take a little Gravy, Anchovy, & butter, & Lemon if you please———

4 rump steaks
Beaten egg
Fresh breadcrumbs mixed with chopped sweet herbs
   (basil, thyme, oregano)
$\frac{1}{2}$ teaspoon anchovy essence
Juice of 1 lemon

Coat the steaks with the beaten egg and then cover with the breadcrumb mixture. Fry in a little hot butter until the steaks are cooked to your taste and the breadcrumb coating is crisp. Keep the meat warm. Melt a bit more butter and scrape up the pan juices. Add the lemon juice and anchovy essence.

# To draw gravey

Take some slices of buttock Beife hack it w$^{th}$ y$^e$ back of a Knife y$^n$ put it into a frying pan fry them with a little fresh buter just enough to brown y$^m$ then put in a pint of water a bunch of sweet hearbs an oynion a little whole pepper & 2 or 3 anchoveis so let it stew leisurely over ye fire till half y$^r$ licquor is wasted y$^n$ squeese out the juce of y$^e$ meat between 2 trenchers and keep it for your use———

4 slices of beef      A bunch of sweet herbs
Butter      Peppercorns
1 pint (*550ml*) water      Anchovy essence to
1 onion              taste

Brown the beef slices in the butter. Add the rest of the ingredients and boil until the liquid is reduced by half. Drain the meat into a jug and squeeze between two plates to get as much of the juice out as possible.

*This is essentially a beef stock. A cheap cut of beef may be used — shin makes a particularly good stock.*

# To Make a Raggou

Take a neck of Mutton and cut it into Stakes, not too thin nor too thick, fry it till tis almost enough, take it up, pour away that you fryed it in, & clean the pann, put in the meat again with a pretty handsome peice of buttar, when the buttar is melted amongst the meat have a quarter of a pint of Capers minced gross, & some sweet herbs minced, one nutmeg grated, a little salt, one anchovy put all in let it fry a very little time, then have the quantity of half a porringer or better of good Strong broth, and put in the pann before you thick it with Eggs, you must have y:ᵉ yolks of three beat together, with a Spoonfull of white vinagar, you must put the broth in the Eggs together, keep all stirring together till y:ᵘ see the sauce thick enough to hang about the meat, then dish it up, Garnish it with some Sliced Lemon, also squeeze the juice of half a Lemon over it.

6 lamb chops
3 egg yolks
2oz (*60g*) butter
1 dessertspoon white
  wine vinegar
2 teaspoons chopped
  capers

1 teaspoon anchovy
  essence
Mixed herbs
Grated nutmeg
Juice of half a lemon

Fry the chops in a mixture of oil and butter until
browned and cooked. Remove from the pan and keep
warm. Clean the pan and then melt 2oz (*60g*) butter in
the pan and add the capers, herbs, nutmeg and anchovy
essence. Cook for a few moments and then add stock.
Mix in the egg yolks and stir constantly over a low heat
until the sauce thickens. Add the juice of half a lemon
and season to taste. Pour the sauce over the chops and
serve.

*This is nothing like what we should today call a ragout,
but the capers and anchovy make it an unusual and very
tasty dish. You could use neck of mutton, but we
preferred the chops.*

9

# To make a hash of Veal, Mutton, or Lamb

Cut y:ʳ meat in fine thinn peices, put it into a deep dish, season it with a little pepper & salt, put to it the quantity of a handsome ladle full of strong broth, one whole oynion, a little Lemon peal minced very small put in 4 or 5 anchovys sett it on the fier, stirr it often when it is almost ready put in a little sweet butter, & have then ready the yolks of 6 or 7 Eggs dissolved with a little viniger to put in when you put in the butter, stirr the Eggs well at first as they doe not curdle, dish it up hott in a dish w:ᵗʰ sippits about, and the Top of a round Manchett in the middle of the Dish, garnish y:ʳ Dish with fine sifted manchett & lemon sliced upon the meat

1–1½lb (½–¾kg) meat off the bone
1 onion
¼ pint (150ml) stock
3 egg yolks mixed with 1–2 teaspoons wine vinegar

2 tablespoons anchovy essence, or to taste
2oz (60g) butter
Grated peel of half a lemon

Melt the butter in the pan and fry the onion gently until soft, then brown the meat cut into small pieces. Add the stock and anchovy essence. Season with salt and pepper and lemon peel. Simmer until the meat is cooked and then add the egg yolks, which have been mixed with the vinegar. Do not let the sauce boil. When it is thick enough, put into a dish and serve up.

*This can be served with 'sippits' or croutons.*

# To Make
# Scotch-Collops

Take a leg of veal and Cutt it in thin slices and hack it w^th y^e Back of a Knife y^n take half a dozen of y^e largest of y:^m and lard y^m well and fry y^m w^th fresh butter tell they are brown y^n put y^m between 2 dishes and set y^m before y^e fire untill all y^e rest are fry:^d and put between 2 dishes y^n wipe y^r pan Clean put in a reasonable quantitye of fresh butter w^th 3 or 4 spoonfull of Claritt y^n take two or three slices of and oynion minced small one anchovy half a nutmeg a little pepper beaten with y^e nutmeg; and salt a proportionable quantitie mix all these together & put it into y^e pan and hold it over y^e fire till it begin to boyle y^n put all your meat except y^r larded peices into y^e pan & put to it y^e yolks [of] 2 or 3 eggs well beaten in a spoonful or two of wine vinegar Keep it all stiring till it begin to thicken y^e sauce y^n a little shallat to rub y^e dish if you please and put y^r Dish over y^e Coals then take y^e udder of veal stuffed and rosted with some of the sasage meat and put into y^e Dish and pour all y^r meat over it. Garnish you Dish with sauceages and fryd bacon and slices of lemon wring the juce of a lemon over it.

1–1½lb (½–¾kg) leg of
   veal, sliced thinly
1 small onion
3oz (90g) butter
3–4 tablespoons wine
1 teaspoon anchovy
   essence

1 egg yolk, mixed with a
   little wine vinegar
Grated nutmeg
Seasoning

Fry the slices of meat in half the butter until cooked and
brown, then put them in the oven to keep warm. Clean
out the pan and put in the remaining butter, with the
wine and the chopped onion, and simmer for a few
minutes. Put back the meat and add the egg yolk mixed
with a little vinegar. If you find the sauce too thick at
this point you may add a little stock. Keep stirring the
sauce until it thickens, not letting it boil or the egg yolk
will curdle. Serve garnished with grilled chipolatas, fried
bacon and slices of lemon.

*Scotch collops have no connection with Scotland — 'to
scotch' meant to chop, and 'collops' is a corruption of
escalopes.*
   *I thought that the stuffed roasted cow's udder was
rather an unnecessary delicacy for modern tastes, so
omitted it.*

13

# To dress Chickens

## M:ʳˢ Ann's Way

First bone them beginning at the neck & so downward, then take the flesh of the breasts & the flesh of a pinnion with the lean of a Gamon and some of the fatt and some beef suit pound it very well in a mable Mortar with their livers parboil'd, with one Anchovy & grated bread & all sorts of sweet herbs yᵗ y:ᵘ like a shallott and 2 or 3 Mushrooms, season pretty well with pepper & salt & a little nutmegg, & 2 or 3 spoons full of Cream, bind all this with the Yolk of an Egg & a little of the white, soe fill the Insides of y:ʳ Chicken with this, sew up the necks & tye the wings & legs, then boil them in water & a little white wine, a bundle of sweet herbs & a little onion & salt & whole pepper, the sauce must be made w:ᵗʰ a little of the liquor they were boil'd in, and some good gravy, & an Anchovy dissolved in a little white wine vineagar, so thicken it with butter add some mushrooms & any other pickle y:ᵘ like, & pour it on them, garnish y:ʳ dish with barbery's: this quantity of forced meat is but enough for two Chicken——

3–3½lb (1½–1¾kg)
  chicken
1 small onion
1 wineglass of white
  wine
6 peppercorns
1 bayleaf
Bouquet garni or bunch
  of fresh herbs

*Gravy*
¼lb (110g) mushrooms
2oz (60g) butter
Approx. ½ pint (300ml)
  chicken stock

*Forcemeat*
2oz (60g) white
  breadcrumbs
Chicken liver
2oz (60g) butter
2 or 3 mushrooms
1 shallot
1 teaspoon anchovy
  essence
Mixed sweet herbs
1 egg
Seasoning

First prepare the stuffing (forcemeat). Chop the shallot and sauté in the butter. Add the liver, which has been parboiled and pounded in a pestle and mortar, and the mushrooms; cook gently for a few minutes. Put the whole mixture in a bowl and add the breadcrumbs, mixed herbs, anchovy essence and seasoning. Mix and add the egg, having removed a little of the white.

Wipe the inside of the chicken with a damp cloth and put in the stuffing. Either sew up the rear end or put a skewer in it to keep it all together. Put in a saucepan with enough cold water to cover and add the white wine, peppercorns, bay leaf and herbs. Simmer until the chicken is cooked — about 1 hour for a roasting chicken or 2–2½ hours for a boiling chicken.

When the chicken is ready, keep it warm in the oven while you make the gravy. Wipe or peel the mushrooms and slice fairly thinly. Fry gently in the butter until they are soft. Add about ½ pint (300ml) stock and stir, boiling rapidly. Pour into a jug and serve.

*We thought that the stuffing was delicious in this, and transformed a boiled chicken into a very special dish.*

15

# To make
# a chicken pigion
# or rabit pye

Take either and cut them in peices and season it $w^{th}$ pepper mace and nutmeg and salt beaten to gether but small take pullets and boyl and blanch them then cut $y^m$ in peices take lamb stones or sweetbreads slice them and $y^e$ marow bones and put them together and $y^e$ yelks of six eggs boyl hard and Artechoake bottoms and sparagrase or potatos boyld and sliced in $y^n$ take very good puff past and put it into a patty pan or dish slice in a lemon and put in a good deal of butter and bake in a quick oven——

1lb ($\frac{1}{2}kg$) rabbit and/or other meat
2oz (60g) butter
2 hard boiled eggs
2 or 3 artichoke hearts or a few asparagus tips
1 sliced boiled potato

$\frac{1}{4}$ pint (150ml) stock
$\frac{1}{2}$lb ($\frac{1}{4}g$) puff pastry
Half a lemon, sliced
Seasoning of mace, ground nutmeg, salt and pepper

Cut the meat into small pieces, season as above, brown and cook until nearly done (about $\frac{3}{4}$ hour). Put in a pie dish with the hard boiled eggs, potato, artichoke hearts, sliced lemon, butter, stock and seasoning. Cover with pastry and put in a hot oven (400°F, gas no. 6) for 30 minutes to set the pastry. Turn the oven down to 350°F, gas no. 4 and cook for a further 40 minutes. Cover with damp greaseproof paper if pastry gets too brown.

*The artichokes are a particularly happy addition to this pie, and the potato is the only one mentioned in the entire book.*

# How to make y^e sassage meat

Take a little of y^e lean of veal and a
little sueit & sage leaves a small
quantitie of tyme and winter savoury
and a little lean of bacon Chop all this
very small y^n put to it y^e yelks of 2 eggs
and season it with nutmeg
pepper and salt

| | |
|---|---|
| 1 lb ($\frac{1}{2}kg$) veal (pie veal will do if it is lean) | Sage, thyme, winter savoury (if available), chopped finely |
| 3 rashers streaky bacon | |
| 2 small egg yolks | Seasoning |

Mince the meat and season. Add the egg yolks (do not make the mixture too wet or it will be difficult to handle), and mix in the herbs. Shape into sausage shape or flat cakes. Cover with flour and fry in a mixture of oil and butter.

# To Boil
# a Hare in a Gugg

Cutt her in small pieces and season her with a penny
worth of Cloves & mace togeather with a little nutmeg
& peper & salt, rub every piece as you put it into the
Gugg; put about the middel of the Gugg a bunch of
Sweet hirbes & a onion sliced, & one Anchovey, with a
pint of White Wine, or Cyder, put the Gugg into a
kettel of Watter & boyl it 3 hours, lett not the Watter
be above the Gugg, and as the Watter boils away keep
it filld with hott watter, when it have boil'd it's time,
take it up, & pouer the Liquor into a poringer with
butter well mixt with flower, boil it well togeather &
poure it upon the Hare, & squeeze a Lemon over it,
the Gugg must be keep Close Stop'd——

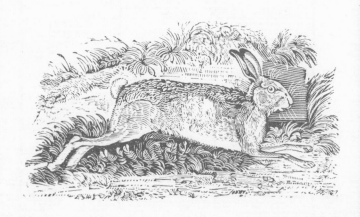

1 large hare
1 sliced onion
Bunch of sweet herbs *or*
  ½ tablespoon dried
  herbs
1½–2oz (*45–60g*) flour

2oz (*60g*) butter
1 pint (*550ml*) wine or
  cider
Seasoning of ground
  cloves, grated nutmeg,
  salt and pepper

Cut the hare into small pieces. Make up a seasoning of
some ground cloves, grated nutmeg, salt and pepper
and sprinkle on each piece of hare. Brown the meat in
some butter in a frying pan and then put in a tall
earthenware pot, with a sliced onion and either a bunch
of fresh sweet herbs or some dried herbs. Pour in the
wine or cider and cover tightly — if the lid does not fit
well, seal with greaseproof paper. Put the pot into a
saucepan of water big enough to have the water at least
two-thirds of the way up the pot, bring up to boiling
point and simmer slowly for 3 hours, replacing the water
as it evaporates.

  When it is cooked, melt the butter in another pan and
add the flour, stirring for a few minutes. Pour in the
juices from the hare and keep stirring until the gravy
thickens. Pour over the hare and dish up.

*This is particularly tasty and much recommended.*
*Contrary to what is usually claimed we found it better*
*on the first day.*

# Sauce to
# a Haunch of Venison

Half a pint of Clarett or Syder 2 anchovies dissolved in it 2 shallotts or a small oynion shread very small & a small bundle of Lemon thyme for a relish a little pepper with this, take off the driping of the flowerd meat not too thick & what Gravy there is this taken off the fier add to it a shread nuttmegg——

| | |
|---|---|
| 1 venison joint, larded with belly of pork | 1 tablespoon flour |
| ½ pint (*300ml*) red wine | 2 teaspoons anchovy essence |
| 1 small onion | Grated nutmeg |

Lard the joint of venison with the pork and cover with foil. Roast in a moderately hot oven (375°F, gas no. 5) allowing 35 minutes per pound. About ½ hour before it is finished remove the foil to brown the joint.

When it is cooked keep the joint warm and make the sauce. Scrape up the pan juices and add the chopped onion, frying gently for a few minutes until soft. Stir in the flour, and then the wine, anchovy essence and thyme. Cook gently, stirring all the time, until thick. Grate on some nutmeg, pour into a jug, and serve with the venison.

# Fish

# To Stew Carps

## *Lady Lear*

Take your carps scale and scower them with salt, then open them take care you doe not break the Gill nor spill the blood and stirr y^e Blood w:^th a little white wine vineagar put y:^r fish into a stewpan & put to them a quart of claret, an onion stuck with cloves 2 or 3 blades of mace a peice of nutmeg a bundle of sweet herbs a shallot or 2, so sett it on a quick fire when it has stew'd a pretty while take a little clarified Buttar made brown with clarifying and pour on the sides of them and when they are stew'd enough take some of the same liquor w:^th some anchovy & butter be sure the sauce is thick enough pour it over the fish garnish y:^r dish w:^th the spawn of the Carp boil'd & what you think fitt————

3½–4lb (*1¾–2kg*) carp
½ pint (*300ml*) white wine
½ pint (*300ml*) water
1 onion stuck with cloves

2oz (*60g*) butter
1 teaspoon anchovy essence
Bunch of herbs
Grated nutmeg
2–3 blades of mace

Clean the fish and scale it. Wash it well in running cold water as this fish tends to be very slimy. When it is washed rub it all over with salt. Put it in a large pan with the white wine, water, onion, herbs, spices and seasoning. Simmer it gently until it is cooked, about 8–10 minutes per pound. Take fish out and keep warm.

In another pan melt the butter until it is brown, then pour in approximately ½ pint (*300ml*) of the liquor the fish was cooked in. Add the anchovy essence. Stir and cook until the sauce is fairly thick. Pour over the carp and serve.
*Serves 6–8*

*This tastes particularly delicious — but I have to admit that I could not face using the blood.*

# To Roast Mackrill

When y:$^r$: Mackrill are open'd & wash't put a pudding in to their bellys made with mackrill Herbs and swet Herbs some Crumbs of Bread yelks of Eggs peper salt nitmeg and butter so make it up in a paist & sew it up in thire bellyes butter a Dripping Pan & Lay them in it before y$^e$ fire turning them as Occation requires baste them with butter & strew some salt on y:$^m$: and some flower w:$^n$ they are allmost done enough strew some shrid herbs and Crumbs of bread on them you must make the sause with Gravey Clarett Anchovies onion peper salt and the pudding that was roasted in the mackrill some juce of Lemon and thicken it with butter

24

4 mackerel
4oz (*110g*) fresh
   breadcrumbs
2 egg yolks
1 onion
1 tablespoon anchovy
   essence

½ pint (*300ml*) wine
Sweet herbs
Grated nutmeg
Juice of 1 lemon
Seasoning

Clean the fish and remove their heads. Put the
breadcrumbs into a bowl and add some sweet herbs,
grated nutmeg and seasoning. Mix in the egg yolks to
make a paste. Put the stuffing into the stomachs of the
fish. Butter a shallow dish, put in the fish and dot with
butter. Cook in a moderate oven (375°F, gas no. 5),
basting often. When they are nearly cooked — about 20
minutes — put some sliced onion over the fish, and
some more breadcrumbs and herbs. Return to the oven
for about 15 minutes longer.

Keep the fish warm in the oven while you make the
sauce. Scrape up the pan juices and add the anchovy
essence, wine, lemon juice and seasoning. If you need
to, thicken with some knobs of butter.

# To Pot Mackerell, Pilchards or Herrings

Take 3 Dozen of Mackerell that are not very large, gutt them and wash y^m very clean, & dry y^m in a Cloath & take off their heads then take a handfull of salt, a quarter of an ounce of Pepper, a Dozen Cloves, a Nutmegg, beat y^r spice and mix that and your salt together & season y^r fish one by one inside & out, & lay them close in y^r Pan then Pour on them 3 quarters of a pint of vinigar, some people add a little Clarret, then put them into an Oven after a Batch of household bread is drawn, and lett y^m stay in it all Night, you may cover y^r Pan w^th Paste, or only tye Severall Sheets of Paper close over it, you must not open the Pot till it is quite cold——

4 mackerel
¼ pint (*150ml*) wine
    vinegar
Small wineglass of white
    wine or cider

Cloves
Nutmeg
Seasoning

Clean and head the fish and wash thoroughly. Put in a dish and season with the spices and salt and pepper. Pour over the vinegar and wine or cider and cover well with baking foil. Bake for 30–45 minutes in a moderate oven (350°F, gas no. 4). Serve warm or cold.

*These taste like soused mackerel, and are very good.*

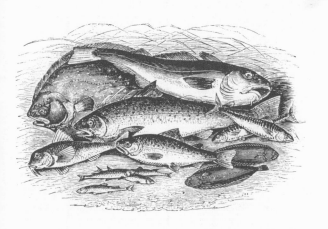

# To marinate Fish
# the best way

## Mr Cary

First fry y:ʳ fish very well & brown in the best oyle can
be gott, the oyle must be so hott y:ᵗ it leave hissing &
boile quietly before you put in your fish (observe if y:ʳ
fish be in season 'twill soon fry the flower on top of it
Crisp) Then make y:ʳ pickel thus, take as much
vineagar as will cover y:ʳ fish, to the quantity of two
quarts of pickle put in a small handfull of salt two penny
worth of saffron a little gross peper, of Cloves and
Cinamon and small quantity, 3 or 4 sprigs of Rosemary
and a few bay leaves. let it boil half or quarter of an hour
at most, then let it be cold, & then put in y:ʳ fish &
slice in some lemon to it, y:ʳ fish must be cooling 10 or
12 hours before it be put into the Pickel. If y:ʳ vineagar
be very strong y:ᵘ must put in some wine to the boiling
the Pickel.

Use no salt but in the Pickell only, & but very few bay
leaves. To be served in w:ᵗʰ some of the Pickel and
eaten with Oyle. If you barrell it y:ᵘ must put a little
oyle on the top.


The fish that are best to Marinate are salmon cut in
pieces through the thickness of them, Troutes, Soles,
Lamprys, Mackrel, Eeles, Smelts, Breames, and all
other firme fish are fitt to be used in this kind.

The fish must be gashed & sprinkled w:ᵗʰ flower, before
it be fryed——

4 whole fish or steaks
  (see above)
Flour
Oil

*For the marinade*
$\frac{1}{4}$ pint (*150ml*) wine
  vinegar
$\frac{1}{4}$ pint (*150ml*) white
  wine

1 lemon
1 small onion
A pinch each of saffron,
  ground cloves and
  cinnamon
Sprig of rosemary
1 bay leaf
Salt and freshly ground
  pepper

Dredge the fish in flour, having first gashed the skin if
you are using whole fish, and brown quickly in hot oil.
Reduce the heat until cooked through. Leave to cool.

  To make the marinade, boil all the ingredients gently
for about $\frac{1}{4}$ hour. Allow to cool, then place fish in a dish
with a lid, pour over marinade and add half a sliced
lemon. Cover and leave for at least 12 hours, turning
several times. Drain the fish and serve with sliced lemon
and onion rings.

*This makes an excellent fish starter.*

# To Make
# Sauce for fish

Take Gravy a little vineagar 3 or 4
Spoonsfull of Grated Bread, 3 Anchovys
& a little horse reddish & whole pepper,
2 or 3 blades of mace a little lemon peel
beat altogether till there be liquor
enough to make it boyle then
draw up y:ʳ butter

4 mackerel (or other oily
   fish)
1 tablespoon wine
   vinegar
1 tablespoon anchovy
   essence
1 teaspoon grated
   horseradish

4 tablespoons grated
   breadcrumbs
Grated lemon peel
2–3 blades of mace
Butter
Seasoning

Mix the breadcrumbs, vinegar, anchovy essence,
horseradish, mace, lemon peel, salt and pepper in a
bowl. Clean and head the fish, and spread with the
breadcrumb mixture. Fry in butter until well cooked;
serve immediately.

*This did not work too well as a sauce, so I adapted it as
above and found it most successful.*

30

# Vegetables

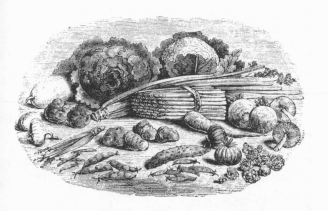

# To Make
# Pease Pottage

*Lady Lear*

Take a quart of strong broth the flower of a pint
of Pease one ox pallet or balls of forced meat,
sett these over a Chafin dish of coals season it
with Mace & Pepper let it boyl a quarter of an
hour then put into it a handfull or two of
spinage & as much sorrel let it boyl a little
longer then put in a little spare-mint half a
pound of butter let it stand over the fire till
thick then serve it up———

12oz (*370g*) peas,
  frozen or fresh
1 pint (*550ml*) chicken
  stock
4oz (*110g*) each,
  spinach and sorrel*

4oz (*110g*) butter
Mace
Mint
Seasoning

Boil the peas hard in the stock with the salt, pepper and mace, 15 minutes for fresh peas, 5 minutes for frozen. Add the spinach and sorrel, finely chopped, and cook for a further 5–10 minutes. Put in some chopped mint and stir in the butter until it has melted. Leave it cooking slowly until it is very thick. Serve as a vegetable.

*If you cannot get sorrel, use double the amount of spinach.

*This is surprisingly tasty and makes a most interesting accompanying vegetable.*

# To Stew Mushrooms

Take y:$^r$ mushrooms & peal them & put 'em into water & salt them & when they have layn a little while put 'em into a Cullendar a draining, then sett 'em over y:$^r$ fier in an Earthen pipkin with a hard crust of bread & a little salt & let 'em stew in their own Liquor till they are pretty tender w:$^{ch}$ will be in a little time: y:$^n$ take out the bread & liquor if there be any, y:$^n$ put to them as much Clarrett as y:$^u$ think fitt, with a few sweet herbs & a shallot or two minced small & a little spice tyed up in a rag, when all y:$^s$ is stewed enough, add to it a little thick melted buttar:

8oz (*250g*) mushrooms
$\frac{1}{4}$ pint (*150ml*) wine
1 small sliced onion
Mixed herbs

Peel the mushrooms and soak in salted water for about an hour. Drain well and put in a pan with a little salt and a hard crust of bread (to soak up the juices). Cover and stew very gently until the mushrooms are tender, about 10 minutes. Strain them and remove the crust. Add the wine and the onion, and sprinkle with a mixture of herbs. Boil gently for about another 10 minutes. Add a small knob of butter and serve up.

*These taste quite sharp, and make a pleasant change to sweated mushrooms.*

# Desserts

Printed for Rich: Chiswell

# To Make Burnt Cream

Take a large pint of Cream sett it over the fire with a blade or two of Mace and a little Cinnimon, then take the yolks of three Eggs and a little flower and some sugar and a little cold Cream to mix it, when the Cream boyls put in your Eggs stirring it till it boyles again, then take it off and put it into the Dish that you send to the table, when it is Cold sift a little fine sugar over it and hold a hott Iorn over it till it is brown, take care it doe not turn in the boyling

½ pint (*300ml*) each, single and double cream
3 egg yolks
2oz (*60g*) castor sugar

1 teaspoon flour
½ teaspoon cinnamon
2–3 blades of mace
Demerara sugar

Bring the cream to the boil with the mace. In another bowl mix the egg yolks, flour, sugar, cinnamon and a little cold cream and put in the top of a double-boiler. Cook slowly, stirring all the time and making sure the mixture does not boil, until it thickens. Strain into a dish and leave to cool, then chill.

Sprinkle the demerara sugar fairly thickly on top of the custard and put under a hot grill, turning all the time to melt and brown the sugar evenly. When the sugar has melted, put back in the fridge at once to set.

# M^rs Rupe's Lemon Cream

Take 5 large lemons wring out all the juice y:^n ke y^e rinde of one lemon pared very thinn & put it in the juice w:^th as much fine sugar as will make it very Sweet set it on a quick fire make it boyling hot but not boyl, then have ready the whites of 5 eggs well beaten & y:^e treads* taken out, put them in the juice of Lemon stirring it, y:^n take it presently off the fire & Strain it throw a flannel jelly bag set it on a quick fire always stirring it, let it boyl when you see white scum or froth rise about the sides 'tis enough put it in w:^t you will serve it in it will jelly & look white & clear you may add a spoon full or two of water to the juice 'twill mend the Colour

3 large lemons
4–6oz (*110–180g*) sugar
3 egg whites

Pare the skin of one of the lemons and put in a pan with the juice of all the lemons. Dissolve the sugar in the juice over a low heat. Add the whisked whites of 3 eggs and stir over low heat for a few minutes. Strain the mixture through a jelly bag and let it cool.

*Seventeenth-century cooks seem to have had an aversion for the threads (sometimes called 'cocks threads') in eggs — many of the recipes recommend their removal.

# To make a sillubub

*Curd on y<sup>e</sup> top*
*Cream in y<sup>e</sup> midle*
*clear in y<sup>e</sup> Bottome*

Take y<sup>e</sup> whites of 4 or 5 eggs and beat them to
a froth with a whisk both ends tyed together
then put in near half a pound of double refin<sup>d</sup>
sugar then put in the juce of a lemon and beat it
till the sugar be melted then put in half a pint of
good Cream and sack beat together be sure it
be sweet enough then beat altogether a good
while soe put it into Clear glasses and let it
stand six hours at least before you sett it to y<sup>e</sup>
table beat y<sup>r</sup> sugar and strain y<sup>r</sup> lemon

4–5 egg whites
8oz (*250g*) castor sugar
Juice of a large lemon
½ pint (*300ml*) double cream
4 teaspoons sweet sherry

Whisk the egg whites until they are very stiff. Slowly
add the lemon juice and the sugar. Continue to whisk
until this mixture is very thick, then add the cream and
sherry, whisking all the time. Pour into individual dishes
or one large bowl and leave for at least six hours.

*When this has stood you will find that it has separated*
*as the title suggests — and that it is quite delicious.*

## LVIII.

A Feaſt.        *Convivium.*

| When a Feaſt | Cum apparatur |
|---|---|
| is made ready, | *Convivium,* |
| the Table is covered | Menſa ſternitur |
| with a Carpet 1 | *Tapetibus* 1. |
| and a Table-Cloth 2. | & *Mappâ,* 2. |
| by the Waiters, | à *Triclinariis,* |
| who beſides | qui prætereà apponunt |
| lay the Trenchers, 3. | *Diſcos* (Orbes) 3. |
| Spoons, 4. | *Cochlearia,* 4. |
| Knives, 5. | *Cultros,* 5. |
| with little Forks, 6. | cum *Fuſcinulis,* 6. |
| Table-Napkins, 7. | *Mappulas,* 7. |
| Bread, 8. | *Panem* 8. |

with

# To Make y^e boyl'd Chocolate Cream

take a pint of Cream and boyl it and half a quarter of a p:^d of chocolate finely scraped put it into a porringer and wh^n y^r Cream is a little cold with a spoon put some of it by degrees to y^r Chocolate stir and disolve it by degrees and then put in more Cream into y^e skillet mix it very well w:^th a chocolate mill put in orange flower water and fine loafe sugar to y^r tast still milling of it well together then put in y^e whites of 2 eggs well beaten and mill it to a high froth take it off by spoonfulls & putt it into little China Cups and heap it up if y^o have a mind to have some in y^e bottome to drinke put it in first & lay froth on it if the froth hold not out put another white of an egg beaten——

¼ pint (*150ml*) each, single and double cream
2oz (*60g*) melted chocolate
2 egg whites
2–4oz (*60–110g*) castor sugar
2 tablespoons orange flower water

Boil the cream and stir in the melted chocolate, mixing all the time. Add the sugar and orange flower water. Let this cool a bit, whisk the egg whites until stiff, and spoon into individual bowls. Pour over the hot chocolate sauce and serve.

*This pudding was a great success. I feared that the egg whites would be very bland, but with the hot chocolate sauce over them they are wonderful.*

# To make
# a Chockalate Cream

Take a quart of cream and a quarter of a
pound chocolate grate it very fine $y^n$
mix $y^r$ Cream and it together season
with sugar and orange flower water to
$y^r$ tast then mill it till it is very thick and
pour into $y^r$ Dishes———

½ pint (*300ml*) double cream
4oz (*110g*) plain chocolate
3 teaspoons orange flower water

Melt chocolate in a bowl over a pan of hot water. When
it has melted let it cool for a few minutes, then stir it into
the cream. Add the orange flower water and stir until
the mixture is thick. If it goes too thick, add a little
single cream to thin it.

*This is the consistency of a mousse, and very rich. I left
out the sugar that MC advised as I felt it was sweet
enough.*

# Welch Pancakes

Take a pint of Cream eight Eggs four Spoonfuls of Brandy, a Nutmeg a Quarter of a pound of Sugar 3 ounces of melted butter, & flour to Make it as thick as Common pancakes butter the pan for the first Pancake then the fry themselves, Steep a littel oreng peal in the Brandy it is very good

$\frac{1}{4}$ pint (*150ml*) single
  cream
2 eggs
1oz (*30g*) castor sugar
1oz (*30g*) melted butter

6 tablespoons flour
1 tablespoon brandy
Grated orange peel
  steeped in brandy or
  cointreau

Mix the cream, eggs, brandy, sugar and butter. Then slowly add the sifted flour, beating until thick. Heat some butter in a pan until smoking hot, then pour in about a coffee cupful of the pancake mixture. When it is cooked on one side, flip it to the other. The pancake should be brown and crisp.

Steep a little grated orange peel in brandy or cointreau, and pour over the cooked pancakes.

*These are richer than normal pancakes, and the orange topping is, as MC says, 'very good'.*

# To Make
# an Apple Pudding

Take 7 or 8 Midling Apples that are pritty
sharp & stew them so soft as to strain them
through a Range & whilst it is hott stir into it
half a pound of Butter and half a pound of Sugar
then beat 8 Eggs whites & all the peels of 2
Lemons grated and mix it all togeather & put
it in a Dish with a sheet of Puff Paste
under an Hour Bakes it

4 cooking apples, peeled
    and cored
3oz (*90g*) butter
4oz (*110g*) sugar

4 egg whites
8oz (*250g*) puff pastry
Grated lemon peel

Peel, core and slice the apples and cook them gently in
a little water until very soft. Add sugar and butter and
beat until it is all well mixed; add the lemon peel. Whip
the egg whites until stiff and then fold into the apple
puree. Pour into a pie dish and cover with puff pastry.
Make two slits in the top and brush with milk. Bake in a
moderately hot oven (400°F, gas no. 6) for 20–30
minutes.
    Serve warm with cream.

# New Coll Puddings

Take 3 half penny worth of white Bread* grated half a
pound of Beef suett minced small half a pound of
Currants a nutmeg and a littel salt, as much Cream &
3 Eggs as will make it almost as stiff as past then make
it in the fashion of an egg and put them into a dish or
stewe pan melting first in it a quarter of a pound of
Butter sett the puddings over a Clear fire & turn them
till they are brown all over, for the sauce take Sack Sugar
& rose watter and Butter you may add swettmeat if you
pleas when you Dish them up strew some fine Sugar
over them——

4oz (*110g*) grated
   breadcrumbs
4oz (*110g*) suet
4oz (*110g*) currants
4oz (*110g*) melted
   butter
2 small eggs
Grated nutmeg

*For the sauce*
2 tablespoons sugar
2 teaspoons rose water

Mix the breadcrumbs, suet and currants together; add
nutmeg and a pinch of salt. Mix in the eggs to form a
stiff paste — add a little cream if it needs to be wetter.
Melt the butter in a pan and put in the mixture, shaped
like an egg, to fry gently until browned and crisp,
turning when necessary.

   For the sauce, add the rose water and sugar to the
pan and stir until the sugar has melted. Pour over the
pudding and serve hot with cream.

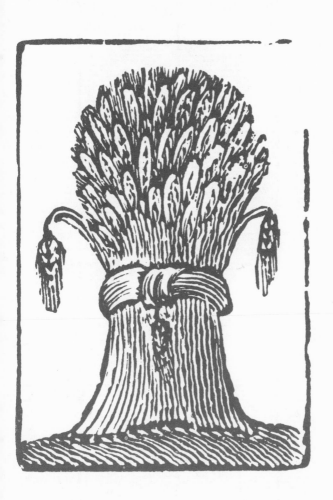

\*The normal 2lb loaf cost 2*d* in MC's day; I have
reduced the amount of breadcrumbs used.

*This is a rather superior bread and butter pudding.*

# To make
# a brown bread Pudding

*Mrs Stringer*

Take 2 good double handsfull of brown bread
grated & one spoonfull of flower $\frac{1}{2}$ a pound of
beefe suit $\frac{1}{2}$ a pound of Currance 1 nuttmegg
grated 2 spoonsfull of sugar 5 Eggs well beat as
much milk as will temper it pretty soft, tye it up
in a cloth let it boyle an hour & $\frac{1}{2}$, let the sauce
be a little sack, Rose water, sugar
& a little fresh butter

4oz (*110g*) grated
  breadcrumbs
2oz (*60g*) flour
8oz (*250g*) currants
8oz (*250g*) suet
2oz (*60g*) castor sugar
4 small eggs
Milk
Grated nutmeg

*For the sauce*
2oz (*60g*) butter
2 tablespoons sugar
2 tablespoons sweet
  sherry
2 tablespoons rose water

Mix all the dry ingredients together. Stir in the eggs and
a little milk if the mixture is too dry. Put it into a greased
bowl and cover with a cloth or greaseproof paper with
foil on top. Boil steadily for 1–1½ hours.

   To make the sauce, melt the butter, add the sherry and
rose water. Stir in the sugar and keep stirring until it is
all well mixed and the sugar dissolved. Turn the
pudding out on to a dish and pour the sauce over it.
Serve hot with cream.

*We thought this was very good; it is much lighter than
the normal suet pudding.*

47

# To Make
# an Orange Pudding
## *Mrs Stringer*

Take a pound of butter & melt it very thick, a pound of white sugar sifted very well and y$^e$ Yolks of 12 Eggs beaten very well, take out the Cocks treads: w:$^n$ y:$^r$ Eggs are beaten very well, put in the Melted butter & sugar beating in well together, then take a whole Candied Orange Peel cut it as small as mincemeat & put it in keep it beating till y:$^r$ paste is made & the oven ready to bake in, make puff paste and bake it in a pewter Dish with Crust under & over it let it stand in the oven about a quarter of an hour

4oz (*110g*) butter
2–4oz (*60–110g*) castor
  sugar
3 egg yolks

8oz (*250g*) puff pastry
Grated rind of 1 orange
1 teaspoon orange
  flower water

Melt the butter and add the sugar, stirring over a low heat until the sugar has dissolved. Beat the egg yolks until very thick, then slowly beat in the butter and sugar and go on beating until the mixture is thick and smooth. Add the orange peel and orange flower water.

Divide the pastry into two parts. Roll out one half and put in a greased pie dish, pour in egg and orange mixture and cover with remaining pastry. Brush with milk and bake in a fairly hot oven (400°F, gas no. 6) for 15–20 minutes. Eat warm.

The contrast between the pastry crust and the creamy inside of this pudding is wonderful. We found it slightly sweet, and I should recommend the smaller quantity of sugar. I also strongly recommend the use of an electric mixer.

# Butterd Oranges

Take 5 Oranges pare y:$^m$, y$^n$ boyl y:$^m$
& mash y:$^m$ and pick out all y$^e$ seeds
take 5 Eggs and beat y:$^m$ and a peice
of butter ab:$^t$ y$^e$ bigness of a Walnut, as
much sugar as will season it to y$^e$ tast,
mingle these together set y:$^m$ ˙on y$^e$
fire till it is thick, y:$^n$ take it offe & let
it cool, strew sugar upon it, & sarve it up

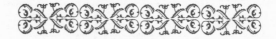

3 oranges
3 eggs
2–3oz (*60–90g*) sugar
½oz (*15g*) butter

Peel the oranges, cut into slices and put them into a
saucepan. Stir over a low heat, mashing them into a
pulp — remove the pith and any pips. Stir in the butter
Whisk the eggs and sugar and add to the orange
mixture. Stir over a low heat until the mixture thickens.
Pour into a dish and eat cold.

# Cakes
# and biscuits

# To Make Bunns

*Lady Lear*

Take a pound of butter & melt it, & a quart of
Cream stirr it till it comes pretty thick then put
it with y:ʳ butter and beat 3 eggs with a little
sack & a little spice & a pint of ale yeast &
continue whipping it up then cutt in y:ʳ flower
& when it is as thick as you think fitt putt in
y:ʳ currants well washed & dry'd
half an hour will bake them.

| | |
|---|---|
| 2oz (*60g*) butter | 6oz (*180g*) flour |
| ¼ pint (*150ml*) each, | 4oz (*110g*) castor sugar |
|    double and single | 6oz (*180g*) currants |
|    cream | 2 teaspoons sherry |
| 1 egg | 2 tablespoons beer |

Melt the butter. Whip the cream until quite thick, then
pour in the butter. Beat the egg with the sherry and
then, stirring all the time, add to the cream and butter.
Put in the beer, currants and sugar and beat well. Fold
in the sifted flour and put into greased tins. Bake in a
moderate oven (375°F, gas no. 5) for 25–30 minutes.

Makes 24 cakes.

*These cakes are delicious. I added sugar as the mixture
seemed a little sour without it. Maybe sack and
seventeenth-century ale were very sweet and therefore
took the place of sugar in this recipe.*

# To Make
# M^rs Mohns Ginger Bread

Take 4 pound of Flower & 2 p^d of treacle & 1
pound & half of Butter and one pound of sugar,
and one ounce of Carraway seeds and 2 ounces
of Ginger, and a quarter of a pint of milk, first
mix y:^r Treacle & flower well togeather, then
melt y:^r Butter in y^e milk and mix the other
things with it, then make a hole in the midle
and power it in & lett it stand whilst y:^r oven is
heting which must be so hot as for manched,
Bake it upon tin plats well Butter'd——

1lb ($\frac{1}{2}kg$) flour
6oz (*180g*) butter
4oz (*110g*) sugar
8 tablespoons black
   treacle

$\frac{1}{2}$oz (*15g*) ground ginger
$\frac{1}{4}$oz (*8g*) caraway seeds
2–4 tablespoons milk

Mix the flour and treacle together. Melt the butter in the
milk and add the sugar, ginger and caraway seeds. Stir
until well mixed. Pour slowly into the flour mixture,
stirring all the time. Pour into a greased cake tin and
bake in a slow oven (325°F, gas no. 3) for 1 hour.

*This is really more like a chewy biscuit and is very spicy.*

# The little hollow Biskett

*Lady Lear*

Take 6 eggs & a spoonfull of rose water beat 'em together very well, $y^n$ put in a pound & 2 ounces of sugar beaten & sifted stirr it till 'tis well mix'd $y{:}^n$ put in as much flower as will make it thick enough to lay out in drops on sheets of white paper, stirr it together till the flower be well mix'd, $y{:}^n$ drop it on white paper & beat a little loaf sugar & sift over them, & bake 'em in an oven not too hott, as soon as them are baked whilst hot pluck 'em off the paper & putt 'em in a sieve & sett 'em in the oven $w{:}^n$ its almost cold $w{:}^n$ they are dry they are for use——

8oz (*250g*) castor sugar
Approx. 8oz (*250g*) plain flour
3 eggs
1–2 tablespoons rose water

Whisk the eggs, rose water and sugar until very thick. Add the flour to dropping consistency. Put spoonfuls on a greased tray, sprinkle with castor sugar, and bake in a moderate oven (350°F, gas no. 5). Cook for 20 minutes or until golden brown. Take off the tray and put on a rack at the bottom of a cool oven to dry.

Makes 24 biscuits.

# To make biskett
# my lady napeirs way

A pound of double refined sugar and 12 eggs yolks &
whites soe whip them up with a birchen rod to a froth,
& as the froth rises cast it into the sugar so continue
beating the sugar & Eggs together, till all the froth is in,
& beat it one hour, then sift in one pound of flower,
w:ch has been well dryed in an oven after household
bread has been drawn, beat it all very well together
half an hour, then let y:r oven be pritty quick but not
scorching, y:n have y:r platts ready butter'd very thin,
& putt in a good full spoonfull in each Plate, & y:n
putt 'em into the oven & w:n they are rise up to top &
a little co ler'd take 'em out w:th a sharp knife & put
'em in again to the oven to harden

---

4oz (*110g*) castor sugar
4oz (*110g*) flour
3 eggs

Heat the oven to 375°F, gas no. 5. Whisk the eggs until
frothy and light. Slowly pour in the sugar whisking all
the time; continue until the mixture again becomes very
light. Add the sifted flour and beat the mixture until it is
very smooth. Pour into small greased cake tins and cook
for 15–20 minutes, or until they are risen and firm to the
touch.

When they are cooked take them out of the tins with a
sharp knife, and if you want them very crisp put them in
a cool oven and bake them until they are hard.

Makes 24 biscuits.

# To make Apricok Cakes

Take your Apricocks w:$^n$ they are just ripe scald y$^m$ till they are soft, & do rise to y$^e$ top of y$^e$ water w:$^n$ they are tender enough to mash abroard take y:$^m$ very clean from the water, y:$^n$ stone y;$^m$ & take out y$^e$ strings very clean y:$^n$ take near y$^e$ weight of y$^e$ pulp by itself in sugar & boyl y$^e$ pulp by itself till with stirring it you may see y$^e$ bottom of y$^e$ skillet pretty plain, y$^n$ put in y$^r$ sugar by degrees & all y$^e$ while y$^e$ pulp is boyling you must stirr it & also while y$^e$ sugar is putting in, & w:$^n$ y$^e$ sugar is all in let it just boil & y:$^n$ take it offe, you may know w:$^n$ it is boiled enough if you take a little of it in a spoon if it is ready their will arise a little thin crust arriving over it: w:$^n$ y$^e$ have taken it offe y$^e$ fire put it in a bason, & let it stand therein a day or two & y:$^n$ lay it out in little Cakes on a pye plate & so let y:$^m$ dry for 2 or 3 days y:$^n$ double them & dry y:$^m$

8oz (*250g*) dried apricots
Sugar

Soak the dried apricots overnight in enough water to allow them to swell. Boil them in the same water until they are very tender — about 10–15 minutes. Drain them, mash them hard and weigh them. Put the apricots in a pan and bring the pulp to the boil. Add the same weight of sugar as pulp, stirring constantly. When the sugar has dissolved boil rapidly until it is very thick, as in making jam. You will know when it is ready by testing like jam on a cold plate, but it must set much quicker than a jam.

Pour into a bowl and leave it for 2 days. Then put teaspoonfuls of the mixture on a baking sheet and bake them in a slow oven for about an hour. Take them out and leave them for about 3 days in a warm dry place, remembering to turn them each day. They are ready to eat when a hard crust has formed all round them.

Makes 24 cakes.

*These taste very like crystallised fruits.*
*You could use 1lb ($\frac{1}{2}$kg) of fresh apricots when in season. Boil them and stone them, taking the bits out, then follow the recipe as above.*

# To make Orange Cakes

Take y$^e$ fairest Oranges you can get cut y:$^m$ in quart:$^{rs}$ & take out their Insides, & put it into a bason, & take out all y$^e$ seeds & skins very clean, & pare y$^e$ rinds as think as you can y$^e$ length of y$^e$ Oranges set them over y$^e$ fire in fair wat:$^r$ & boyl them till they are tender, y$^n$ take y$^m$ up, & mince y$^m$ small, & take y$^e$ weight of y:$^m$ in double refind sugar & boil them to a Candy height, y$^n$ take it offe y$^e$ fire, & put y$^e$ Rinds y$^e$ Insides & sugar all together, then set it over y$^e$ fire & let it boil a little & stirr it when it comes offe, y:$^n$ set it offe in a stove in an Earthen bason, keep fire to it, till it be fit to drop y:$^n$ drop them on Glasses & let y$^m$ dry thereon———

4 oranges
Sugar

Pare the skin off the oranges very thinly and boil it for 10 minutes until tender. Meanwhile take the pith off the oranges (you can do this by pouring boiling water over them and leaving them for a few minutes, when they will peel very easily). Quarter and slice up the fruit, removing any bits of skin, pips, etc.

When the peel is tender, drain off the water and weigh the cooked peel. Measure out the same weight in sugar. Chop up the peel very finely and put in with the sugar. Stir over a low heat until the sugar has melted and then boil hard until it starts to turn brown. Add the orange flesh and continue to boil, mashing it and stirring until most of the liquid has evaporated and the mixture is thick.

Drop small spoonfuls on to greased baking trays and dry in the bottom of a warm oven.

Makes approximately 12 cakes.

*These taste like little dried spoonfuls of marmalade, which is very pleasant if you like marmalade. My six-year-old son found them irresistible.*

# To Make
# yᵉ Duke of York's Cakes

Take one pound of Flower well dry'd, one pound of fresh butter, one pound of fine powder sugar, mix the flower and sugar together 16 eggs leaving out half the whites, beat y:ᵉ Butter in a pan till it comes to Cream, then mix the Eggs with the butter by degrees, and allso the flower, you must keep beating it 2 hours, then put it in to y:ʳ pans & bake them

4oz (*110g*) flour
4oz (*110g*) butter

4oz (*110g*) castor sugar
3 small eggs

Mix the flour and sugar together. Beat the butter until it goes creamy and then slowly add the beaten eggs. Gradually mix in the sugar and flour and beat hard.

Grease some small tins and put in the mixture. Bake in a moderate oven (375°F, gas no. 5) for about 20 minutes.

Makes 18 cakes.

# Preserves

We were not able to test these recipes since the plum season was over, but they are quite straightforward and easy to follow.

For white plums you may use Coe's Golden Drop, Yellow Pershore, or one of the gages — Deniston's Superb or Early Transparent.

Bonum Magnum — a sharp yellow plum much used for cooking and preserving — has only recently died out, and was probably the parent of the modern Yellow Pershore (also known as Yellow Egg), which may be used in its place.

## To Preserve green Plums.

Take your fairest white Plums when they are
green and weigh to them their weight in fine sugar
then put them into scalding water and let them stand
in it tell they will peel then take them out of y hot
water and put them into cold water and peel them then
put them into a skillet of fair water and let them
stand in a scalding heate till they are green they
must not bee in any more water then will just
cover them, then take as much of the water they were
greened in as you count to make a syrup if y think
them not green enough you may heate them 4 or 5
times before y finish them

## To p'serve y Bonum=magnum.

Take a pound of the plums called by that name one
pint of water, 2 pound of sugar, boyl your sugar and
water first and skim it very well then put it to your
plums boyling hot and let them stand 4 or 5 hours
then scald them again, and y next day boyl them up
and put them up for your use

# To make
# Orange Marmalade

Take your oranges, & pair y:ᵐ very thin y:ⁿ cut yᵐ in halves squeeze out yᵉ juice, & take out yᵉ seeds & put their halves to steep 17 hours in water y:ⁿ boyl y:ᵐ in 5 severall wat:ʳ keeping y:ᵐ und:ʳ wat:ʳ till they be very tend:r yⁿ take y:ᵐ out, & lay y:ᵐ on a cloath to dry & take to every p:ᵈ of oranges thus boyl'd a p:ᵈ of double refined sugar y:ⁿ beat yᵉ Oranges to a pulp whilst you boyl your sugar to a Candy yⁿ put yʳ pulp into yʳ sugar & stir it well yⁿ boyl it a quart:ʳ of an hour ov:ʳ a quick fire y:ⁿ put into it 3 quart:ʳˢ of a pint of yᵉ juice wᵗʰ 6 ounces of sugar already disolv'd in it y:ⁿ set it on yᵉ fire & boil it to a Marmalade height then put it into Glasses for your use

The Bermudos Oranges are yᵉ best but for want of these you may use those of Cevil——

6 Seville oranges
Sugar
Water

Peel the oranges thinly. Cut them in half and squeeze out the juice into a bowl to keep, and deseed. Steep the orange halves overnight in cold water to cover. Put the oranges into a pan of cold water, and boil them hard until they are tender, changing the water several times.

_ye sour Orange_

When they are cooked drain them, and dry them with a cloth. Weigh them and then measure the same weight in sugar. Dissolve the sugar in the pan (without water) and boil until it reaches 220°F.

Meanwhile pulp the orange halves, then add the puree to the melted sugar. Boil hard for 15 minutes, stirring frequently. Add the juice of the oranges and boil again to jam setting point. Put in clean warm jars and seal.

Makes approximately 3lb (_1½kg_) marmalade.

_I felt that this was sweet enough and so did not add the further 6oz (180g) sugar that MC recommends._

# To make Jelley of Pippins.

*Pare* your Pippins thin, and cut them in quarters put
them into a skillit w: as much fair water to them as
will but just cover them, sett them on quick fire &
Lett them boyb very fast till they are very tender,
pour it through a Strainer, do not squeez it but lett
it run through of it self: then to a pinte of y.e Liquer
take a pound of double refined Sugar, sett on y.e fire
and let it boyl apace, till it begins to jelley and skim
it often then have ready a Lemmon peel pared thin
and cut in little long slices y.t hath been boyled very
tender in Water 2 or 3 times, changed and y.e juice of
a Lemmon or two stir this into your skillit of jelley
and let it boyl a little, then take it up and put it into
shallow Glasses

2lb (*1kg*) apples (Bramleys if available)
Lemon
Sugar

Peel, core and quarter the apples and put them into a
saucepan with enough water to cover. Boil hard until
the apples are very soft. Strain through a jelly bag and
leave dripping, preferably overnight. Measure the juice
and add the same amount of sugar. Boil hard until
setting point is reached, skimming frequently. When the
mixture is beginning to jell, add the juice of the lemon
and the pared skin sliced very thin.

*The term 'pippin' was used to describe several varieties
of apple raised from seed, to distinguish them from
those (the majority) that came from grafted stock.*

# Wines

# A note on the wine recipes

Time has not permitted the testing (and necessary keeping) of these wines, but their feasibility is assured. We recommend that you adapt them to your own basic wine-making process, which will include using a prepared wine yeast and fermentation jars. (For the beginner, there are many good books on the subject.)

Never use metal utensils when making wine, and be sure that all equipment is sterilised. Use only undamaged fruit and flowers, which should be gathered after the dew has dried but before the sun is too hot.

# To Make Elder Wine

*M:ʳˢ Lower*

Take 20 pound of Malaga raisons pick'd and rub'd
clean but not washed shred them very small, let 'em stand
or steep in 5 gallons of water 10 days then pass the
liquor through a hair seive, have in readyness six pints of
elder-berry juice boiled in a glazed pipkin they doe to
make jelly of Currants in a kettle of Water, put in cold
into the liquor made with the raisons & the water, then
stirr it well together and tunn it into a vessel, y:ᵘ
must not stop it close till it has done Working, let stand
in a Warm place six weeks or two months, then bottled
it and it will keep all the year in a cool place
after 'tis bottled.

5lb (2¼kg) raisins          10 pints (5½ litres) water
1½ pints (850ml)            1 teaspoon dried yeast
  elderberry juice

# To Make
# Currant or Raspberry
# Wine

*M:rs Palmer*

To every three quarts of water there must be
one quart of Currants or Raspberries, but first
you must to every two quarts of water take one
pound of sugar & boyl it half an hour then pour
it boyling hott to your Currants or Raspberries
being well bruised & when it is cold work it
with barm* about two days then strain it
through flannel and barrell it till it be fine,
then bottle it, in yᵉ bottling y:ᵘ may
add a little sugar.

2 pints (*1¼ litres*) currants or raspberries
6 pints (*3½ litres*) water
1 teaspoon dried yeast

*Barm is liquid yeast — actually the froth formed on
top of fermenting malt liquors, also called ale yeast.

# To Make Primrose Wine

## *Lady Lear*

Take a Gallon of Water & a pound of sugar boil it an hour $y^n$ pour it boyling hott on a peck of the flowers clean picked & when cold putt a spoonfull of Ale Yest to it, $w^n$ 'tis wrought Tun it into a barril & add to it the juice of 2 or 3 lemons, stop it close for 3 weeks bottle it afair day putting a lump of sugar

2 gallons (*9 litres*) primrose flowers
1lb ($\frac{1}{2}kg$) sugar
2 or 3 lemons
8 pints ($4\frac{1}{2}$ *litres*) water
1 teaspoon dried yeast

# To Make Lemon Mead

Take 10 quarts of Water and 1 quart of honey 3 pound of the best powdered sugar mix these altogether and set it on the fire & boyl it three quarters of an hour keep it continually scuming, y:$^n$ add six pennyw:$^{th}$ of Cloves and mace, 1 race of Ginger sliced and a branch of rosemary y:$^n$ let it boyl one quarter of an hour longer for double the quantity of this take 12 lemons & cut them in two put y:$^m$ into a vessel of fitt bigness and take the liquor boyling from the fire & pour it into your vessell, when 'tis almost cold take 2 brown toasts spread with good yeast and when it hathe done Working stop it up and in a Weeks time bottle it with a lump of sugar, the Week after drink it——

4 pints (2¼ litres) honey
1½lb (700g) sugar
6 lemons
10 cloves
3 blades of mace

1 piece of root ginger
1 sprig of rosemary
8 pints (4½ litres) water
1 teaspoon dried yeast

# Cures

# Cough in Children

Take rosemary shred it small & pour in a quart
of boyling hott water Stop it close keep it on the
embers six hours then straine it out to a pint of
the Liquor one pound of sugar & boyl it to a
Syrrup be sure to make it strong of the Rosemary, give a spoonfull every night going to bed.

A handful of rosemary          Sugar
2 pints (*1 litre*) water

Cut up the rosemary and pour the boiling water on to
it. Cover and leave in a warm place for several hours,
or overnight. Strain the liquor, and to each pint ($\frac{1}{2}$-
*litre*) add 1lb ($\frac{1}{2}kg$) sugar. Boil until it is syrupy.

*A sweet, aromatic, soothing drink; rosemary has the
added property of inducing sweat.*

# For a Sore throat

Tak powder of Ginger and mix it with
Brandy, stiff enough to spreed on a
Cloth and put it to the throat put a peice
of Muslen betwen or it will
draw it out in pimpels

1 teaspoon ground ginger          2 tablespoons brandy

Mix the ginger with the brandy; spread on a cloth and
wrap round the sore throat.

*This acts as a simple and effective counter-irritant.*

# for a pain in y<sup>e</sup> stomack in young folks

*Mrs Clifford*

Take 2 cevill oranges and put into y<sup>m</sup>
some saffron ther rost y<sup>m</sup> and steep y<sup>m</sup>
in a quart of white wine and Drink half a
pint every morning and walk after it so
Doe till you find good in it probatum est

2 Seville oranges
2 pints (*1 litre*) white wine
Saffron

Cut the oranges in half and sprinkle with saffron.
Bake in a moderate oven for 15–20 minutes. Steep
the oranges overnight in the white wine. Strain into a
bottle, and drink every morning until cured.

*This tastes very good, and I imagine after drinking half
a pint of it in the morning you would not feel a pain
for very long. Saffron is a mild purge.*

# For a Bruse or Strain

Take Mallows Chamomile flowers
Elder flowers of each one hand full boyl
them in two quarts of water to three
pints, when cold add a quart of Vinegar
and a pint of Brandy——
this fermentation must be used twice a
Day as hot as it can be enduer'd it will
prevent comeing to a Sore

1 small handful each,       $\frac{1}{2}$ pint (*300ml*) vinegar
  chamomile flowers,     $\frac{1}{4}$ pint (*150ml*) brandy
  elder flowers, mallow flowers

Boil the flowers in a pint of water. Let it cool, strain into
a jug and add the vinegar and brandy. Apply it as hot as
you can bear it.

*This is a sound — if somewhat extravagant — treatment;*
*the heat will stimulate the flow of blood to the afflicted*
*part, which removes the bruising internally.*

# A very good wash for y^e face

2 ounces of Pearl Barly to 3 pints of water boil it till it comes to a quart then put it to a Spoonfull of Brandy and half a Dram of Camphire and one Lemon

2oz (*60g*) pearl barley
3 pints (*1½ litres*) water
1 tablespoon brandy
Juice of 1 lemon
A few drops of camphor oil

Boil the pearl barley rapidly in the water for 10–15 minutes until the water has reduced by one third. Strain into a bowl and add the brandy, lemon juice and oil of camphor. Allow to cool.

*The pearl barley acts as a softener, the lemon as an astringent — a very good combination for tired skin.*

# Appendix

The pencil-written note on the flyleaf of Mary Chafin's receipt book tells us that she was born at Chettle in 1680 (the parish register gives the date as 1682) and married William Clutterbuck in 1698.

Chettle, on the edge of Cranborne Chase in north-east Dorset, belonged before the Reformation to the abbey of Tewkesbury. At some time in the reign of Elizabeth I the estate was bought by Thomas Chafin, whose family came originally from Wiltshire. The Chafins were thus one of those recently established families who had begun to make their mark on English local life after the extraordinary share-out of land caused by Henry VIII's dissolution of the monasteries.

## The Chafin family

Mary's Chafin grandfather, another Thomas, had fought on the Royalist side in the Civil War and been paroled by the governor of Poole in order to mind his estates; he is described by Lord Shaftesbury as 'a personable well-carriaged man of good estate, wanting neither understanding nor value of himself and an enemy to the Puritan cause.' Mary's father, also Thomas, followed the family's Royalist tradition by commanding a troop of Dorset horse at the Battle of Sedgemore in 1685, when Charles II's bastard son James, Duke of Monmouth, tried and failed to seize the throne from his uncle James II.

Mary was the second daughter in a family of eleven children, of whom seven survived at least to adolescence — a surprisingly high proportion in those days of amateur midwives and high infant mortality. Her forebears had in the course of the preceding century acquired a number of other small estates, and by the time of her birth the Chafins were well established as influential members of the county. At that time each county was a separate entity, with its own social

78

classes, administration and culture. Many of the gentry (landowning families qualified to bear a coat of arms) took little part in national life, despite their overwhelming representation in the House of Commons, but as sheriffs and Justices of the Peace they organised and supervised virtually every aspect of local life, from general elections to the poor laws.

Thomas Chafin, Mary's father, served as MP for Poole during the reign of James II, but it was only after the 'Glorious Revolution' of 1688, in which James was deposed and his daughter Mary and her husband William of Orange were crowned joint sovereigns, that the curtailing of royal independence and the more frequent Parliaments led to any real local involvement in national issues of the day. In 1689 Mary's father was in London, taking a close interest in the party politics of the early years of the new reign, and writing home to his wife that 'the prick-eared party are much troubled at the prorogation [of Parliament] and things seem of better complexion than formerly.'

Mary's mother was Anne Penruddock, whose father, Colonel John Penruddock, was leader of Penruddock's Rebellion in 1655 which attempted to restore Charles II to the throne; although planned on a national scale it was a total failure, and Colonel Penruddock was executed at Exeter. Letters from Thomas Chafin to his wife indicate that the marriage was a success and the children brought up in a secure and happy household. One, written to reassure her just before the Battle of Sedgemore, finishes: . . . give my service to all my friends and blessings to brats [at that stage there were six and Mary was two years old] and let Nancy take true love from her dear Tossey.' A month later he was in London, being presented to James II for his loyalty, and apparently feeling rather out of his depth — 'the whole company gazed on us as somewhat extraordinary and enquired who we were, few of our acquaintance being present.'

79

Mary's brothers were probably sent away to school when they were about eight, by which time they would be able to read and write and would know some arithmetic and grammar. Girls tended to be taught at home and so their level of education was much more varied. Most daughters of the gentry probably learned to read, but writing seems to have been a rarer talent and the spelling even of the well educated was notoriously bad. In this respect Mary's book is surprising, for the majority of the recipes are in a slightly unformed but legible handwriting similar to that on the flyleaf, and are remarkably consistent as to spelling. It would seem that Mary's mother had strong views about the value of education for women.

## Mary's marriage and move to Puncknowle

In 1698, when she was sixteen, Mary married William Clutterbuck, about whose previous life virtually nothing is known except that he came from Exeter and was described by a nineteenth-century Dorset historian as 'a sea-faring man'. William and Mary probably remained in Chettle after their marriage, for the parish register records the birth of four of their children: William, born 1700 and died 1710; Mary, born 1702; Thomas, born 1703 and died 1716; and Ann, born 1704. One is tempted to deduce that William Clutterbuck stayed at home for the first four years of marriage and then returned to sea, for no further children were born until after 1709.

In 1709 the young family moved to Puncknowle in south-west Dorset. William had bought the manors of Puncknowle and Bexington from a branch of the Napier family to whom Mary was distantly related; a bond dated 4 June shows Mary's brother-in-law Thomas Haysome standing surety for him. William and Mary remained at Puncknowle for the rest of their lives. Their son and heir John and their daughters Elizabeth and Arundel were born there, and a Mrs Mary Clutterbuck, a contributor to Mary's book and presumably William's mother, was buried there in 1712. It would seem that William continued his naval career at first — perhaps the reason why he had not established his own household sooner — for Thomas Haysome is found acting as his trustee in 1709 in order to fill the Puncknowle living, which was in the gift of the owner of the estate. By 1712, however, William must have given up the sea, for in that year he served as sheriff of Dorset.

Puncknowle Manor stands today, little changed from when Mary lived there. It was built probably in the sixteenth century, and the Napiers had added a new front in the mid-seventeenth century, making the whole building T-shaped. The new wing has a neatly symmetrical front and a handsome two-storeyed porch, which opens on to a large hall with two vast fireplaces in the Elizabethan style (architectural fashions were particularly slow to change in the West Country). Above the hall are two panelled rooms, which probably served as the family's private living quarters. In the early eighteenth century these were decoratively painted, one with land and sea scenes in a muted shade of brown, the other in pink and green with ornamental foliage and winged cherubs' heads.

It would be nice to think that the Clutterbucks were responsible for this piece of extravagance in their newly acquired home, particularly since one of Mary's contributors, Lady Burlington, was wife to the architect earl who built Chiswick House in London and was among the first to champion the Palladian style of architecture in England. At much this time Mary's brother George was commissioning Thomas Archer to rebuild Chettle House in the English baroque style of Vanbrugh and Hawksmoor, a more suitable residence for someone whose 'great popularity' (according to his tombstone in Chettle parish church) 'procured him the honour of representing this county in Parliament from 1713 to 1747.'

**The contributors**

Mary's marriage to William brought her into contact
with a number of Devon families, which suggests that
the Clutterbucks were of reasonable social standing. By
far the most regular contributor to the book — and
therefore presumably visitor — is Lady Isabella Lear,
wife of Sir Thomas Lear of Lindridge, Devon, a wealthy
baronet and MP for Ashburton from 1701 to 1705. Sir
Thomas himself gave a few recipes for wine-making.
Lady Lear was by birth a Courtenay, one of the first
families of Devon, and the Lady Courtenay whose
recipes appear in Mary's book must be either her
mother, wife of the first baronet of Powderham, Devon,
or her neice, wife of the second baronet. Lady Clifford,
another frequent contributor, was the wife of Hugh
Clifford, second baron Clifford of Chudleigh, Devon,
while Mrs Clifford was probably the Mary Clifford who
married Nathaniel Clutterbuck of the Gloucestershire
branch of the family.

At the same time as they cultivated their Devon
connections, the Clutterbucks seem to have established
themselves in Dorset. The Russell family, earls of
Bedford since 1550, came originally from Kingston
Russell, only a couple of miles from Puncknowle, and
Mary's contributor Lady Russell was probably the wife
of Edward Russell, earl of Orford, the eminent naval
commander who burnt the French fleet at La Hogue in
1692. The Mr Cary who gives a fish marinade recipe
would be Nicholas Cary of Upcerne — about eight miles
from Puncknowle — who in 1716 succeeded William as
sheriff, and Mrs Henly was the wife of Henry Henly,
mayor of Lyme Regis in 1722. Other familiar Dorset
names which appear are the Husseys of Marnhull, the
Fownes of Stepleton and the Martyns of Athelhampton.

It is surprising, particularly since Mary stayed near her
own family after her marriage, that so few of her sisters
feature in the book. Only one — Bridget, married to
Thomas Haysome, William's trustee — is mentioned by

name. Other more distant members of her family are well represented, however. As one delves further into Chafin family history one finds an increasingly complex network of constantly crossing lines, involving many different members of the same families. Although their social circle was geographically wide, extending from Wiltshire and Oxfordshire to Devon, the number of families concerned is small. But Mary's contributors are not wholly limited to county families, and there are a number of recipes from more humble individuals in the neighbourhood of Chettle.

## The end of the story

William and Mary died within a few months of each other in 1719: the cause of their death is not known. The recipe book was presumably inherited with the estate by their oldest surviving son John. He died without children and the estate finally passed to the children of Mary's youngest daughter Arundel, who had married George Frome (rector of Puncknowle and grandson of George Pitt of Shroton), and then to Arundel's grandson the Rev. George Clutterbuck Frome. His marriage to Maria-Sophia, daughter of Edmund Morton-Pleydell of Whatcombe House, Dorset, provided the link with the Bingham family, for Maria-Sophia's sister Emma-Septima married in 1814 Sir George Ridout Bingham of Bingham's Melcombe. The book is believed to have been handed down through the Binghams to Mrs James Young of Portsonachan, Argyll (herself a cook of some note), first wife of Robert Bingham and stepmother of the present owner.

With the marriage of Maria-Sophia's daughter Elizabeth-Arundel, Puncknowle became the property of the Grove-Mansel family, and in the nineteenth century the line becomes too tenuous to follow. Similarly Chettle passed out of Chafin ownership in 1818, on the death of Mary's brother George's last surviving son, William, rector of Lidlinch.

# Index

**Picture Acknowledgements**

Ann Ronan Picture Library: 1, 14, 20, 21, 24, 29, 34, 61, 69, 76.
Mansell Collection: 46, 51, 57.
Mary Evans Picture Library: ix, 5, 7, 10, 23, 27, 31, 39, 62.
Radio Times Hulton Picture Library: 35, 73.